TIMELINES

The War on Terror

David Downing

FRANKLIN WATTS
LONDON • SYDNEY

First published in 2007 by Franklin Watts

Copyright © 2007 Arcturus Publishing Limited

Franklin Watts
338 Euston Road
London NW1 3BH

Franklin Watts Australia
Level 17/207 Kent Street, Sydney, NSW 2000

Produced by Arcturus Publishing Limited,
26/27 Bickels Yard, 151–153 Bermondsey Street, London SE1 3HA

Series concept: Alex Woolf
Project manager and editor: Helen Maxey
Designer: Simon Borrough
Picture researcher: Helen Maxey
Consultant: James Vaughan

Picture credits:
Corbis: cover (Ed Kashi/Corbis), 4 (Bettmann/Corbis), 5 (Reza; Webistan/Corbis), 6 (Reuters/Corbis), 7 (Bettmann/Corbis), 8 (Suhaib Salem/Reuters/Corbis), 9 (Saudi Gazette/Corbis Sygma), 10 (epa/Corbis), 11 (Attar Maher/Corbis Sygma), 12 (Chris Collins/Corbis), 13, 14, 15 (Reuters/Corbis), 16 (Corbis Sygma), 17 (Reuters/Corbis), 19 (Ron Sachs/CNP/Corbis), 20, 21 (Reuters/Corbis), 22 (Patrice Latron/Corbis), 23 (Reuters/Corbis), 24 (Corbis Sygma), 25, 28 (Reuters/Corbis), 29 (Ed Kashi/Corbis), 30, 31 (Reuters/Corbis), 33 (Antoine Gyori/AGP/Corbis), 34 (Reuters/Corbis), 35 (epa/Corbis), 36 (John O'Boyle/Star Ledger/Corbis), 37 (Reuters/Corbis), 38 (Kai Pfaffenbach/Reuters/Corbis), 39 (Fernando Camino/Cover/Corbis), 40 (Peter Macdiarmid/epa/Corbis), 41 (Scotland Yard/Handout/Reuters/Corbis), 42 (Pavel Wolberg/epa/Corbis), 43 (Mohammed Salem/Reuters/Corbis), 44 (epa/Corbis), 45 (Syed Jan Sabawoon/epa/Corbis). Rex Features: 18, 26 (Rex Features), 27 (Kevin Wisniewski), 32 (Sipa Press).

A CIP catalogue record for this book is available from the British Library.

Dewey Decimal Classification Number: 303.6'25

ISBN 978 0 7496 7190 7

Printed in China

Franklin Watts is a division of Hachette Children's Books.

Contents

Execution of Sayyid Qutb

29 AUGUST 1966

On 29 August 1966 Egyptian school inspector Sayyid Qutb was hanged for allegedly plotting to overthrow the state. He was a leading member of the Muslim Brotherhood, which had been founded in Egypt in 1928 with the intention of making Egyptian society more Islamic. During a three-year stay in the USA (1948–51) Qutb became convinced that Western culture, with its emphasis on material progress (having more and more things) and its sexual freedoms, presented a terrible danger to Islamic principles. When the newly independent Egyptian governments of Mohammed Neguib (1952–4) and Gamal Abdel Nasser (1954–69) proved more interested in economic growth than promoting Islam, he began campaigning for their overthrow.

Apart from one brief period of freedom, Qutb spent the last 12 years of his life in prison. During that time he wrote several books outlining his political beliefs. Qutb believed that Western values (which, for him, included the equally materialistic values of socialism and communism) were corrupting Islamic society. Western political influence had to be shaken off, and Western power evicted from the Islamic world. It might take generations, Qutb wrote, but a 'cosmic struggle' between Islam and its enemies was inevitable.

QUTB'S INFLUENCE

After his death, Qutb's influence grew. Western interference in Middle Eastern affairs continued to create resentment amongst the Arab population. In addition, many of the region's pro-Western governments were beset by serious economic and political problems.

Material progress in Egypt – the new Aswan Dam under construction in 1964.

TIMELINE

The success of the 1979 Islamic revolution in Iran (against the country's pro-Western government) was proof to many Muslims that defiance of the West was possible. In 1989, the Soviets finally withdrew from their war in Afghanistan. They had fought in support of pro-Western values and against Islamic values, so their defeat was another victory for Islam against the West. But it was more than that. It was a call to action for thousands of men who shared Qutb's vision of a war against the West.

Commander Ahmed Masoud, one of the leaders of the mujahidin (Islamic guerrilla fighters) in Afghanistan.

CROSS-REFERENCE MUSLIM BROTHERHOOD: PAGES 42–43

Qutb's prescription

'What should be our verdict on this synthetic (artificial) civilization? What should be done about America and the West, given **their overwhelming danger to humanity?** Should we not issue a sentence of death? Is it not the verdict most appropriate to the crime?'
From Sayyid Qutb, *Islam and the Problem of Civilization* (Dar al-Shuruq, 1962).

Murder of Abdullah Azzam

Abdullah Azzam and Osama bin Laden were two of the many Muslims who travelled to Afghanistan in the early 1980s. Both men saw military action, but they also found time, in 1984, to set up the Afghan Service Bureau. This agency recruited men from all over the Muslim world to fight in Afghanistan. Once victory was assured – the final withdrawal of Soviet troops took place in February 1989 – the two men decided to create al-Qaeda, an international force. It would send hardened veterans of the Afghan conflict wherever Muslims were at war with non-Muslims.

A NEW BRAND OF TERRORISM

Terrorism – the use of violence against civilians for political ends – has a long and global history. Some terrorists have been Muslims – many of the Palestinian terrorists of the

Soviet troops wave goodbye to Afghanistan, January 1989.

The Marine barracks bombing

The suicide bombing of the US Marine barracks in Beirut on 23 October 1983 killed 241 US servicemen and one elderly Lebanese man. This attack and others in the period 1982–4 was not a terrorist attack as such – the target and victims were overwhelmingly military – but it inspired militant Muslims, like Osama bin Laden, who wished to use suicide bombers against civilians. Most important of all, the bombers looked as though they had achieved their political objective: after claiming that it would not be intimidated by terrorism, in February 1984 the US government pulled its forces out of Lebanon.

1970s, for example – but there was nothing particularly Islamic about their terrorism. It was a series of suicide attacks on US, Israeli and French positions in Lebanon during the period 1982–4 that signalled the merging of terrorism and Islamic extremism. These attacks were mostly aimed at military personnel, but they set in motion a series of suicide bombings against civilians. According to some interpretations of the Islamic texts, men who sacrificed themselves in this way – as part of the struggle (or *jihad*) against the enemies of Islam – went straight to paradise.

BIN LADEN

Bin Laden favoured the use of such tactics in his war against the West. Azzam, however, believed that Islam prohibited the deliberate killing of women and children. On 24 November 1989, explosives were detonated under the car carrying Azzam and his two sons through the streets of Peshawar, Pakistan. Bin Laden may or may not have been involved – but he was now the undisputed leader of al-Qaeda, and free to choose its tactics.

CROSS-REFERENCE
PALESTINIANS:
PAGES 14–15,
42–43
SUICIDE BOMBINGS:
PAGES 40–41,
42–43

US Marines remove a corpse from the rubble of their bombed Beirut barracks, October 1983.

Al-Qaeda's Declaration of War

On 23 February 1998 al-Qaeda issued a declaration of war against the USA and its supporters. It was, the organization claimed, a defensive war. 'For more than seven years,' the statement read, 'America has been occupying the lands of Islam in the holiest of places, the Arabian peninsula, plundering its riches, dictating to its rulers, humiliating its people, terrorizing its neighbours.' These US 'crimes and sins' were 'a clear declaration of war on God, his messenger, and Muslims'.

SAUDI REJECTION

Osama bin Laden had returned to Saudi Arabia in 1990. Later that year, when the country was threatened by Iraq, he offered to defend it with his force of 5,000 Afghan veterans. The Saudi government refused his offer, preferring to rely on US troops. The arrival of the troops enraged bin Laden, who saw them as 'unbelievers' in the Muslim holy land. Americans, he decided, were the main obstacle to the sort of changes he wanted in the Muslim world. In 1996 bin Laden returned to Afghanistan, where the Islamic extremist movement the Taliban had taken power. He set about reviving the old training camps.

LEADING THE WAR

There were several major terrorist attacks between 1990 and al-Qaeda's declaration of war. The first attack on New York's World Trade Center in 1993 did less damage than the attackers had planned. In 1995 a plot to hijack 12 airliners over the Pacific Ocean was foiled. There were two major bombings in Saudi Arabia in 1995–6, the second of which killed 19 US servicemen. In 1997 a mass shooting killed 58 tourists in the Egyptian city of Luxor.

23 FEBRUARY 1998

Thousands of Muslims attend Friday prayers in Mecca's Grand Mosque, January 2004.

AL-QAEDA AND OTHERS 1990–1998

September 1990	▶ Osama bin Laden's offer of help against Iraq is rejected by the Saudi Arabian government.
February 1993	▶ First attack on New York City's World Trade Center, killing 6 and injuring over 1,000.
January 1995	▶ Plan to destroy 12 airliners over the Pacific Ocean is thwarted.
May 1996	▶ Osama bin Laden moves to Afghanistan.
June 1996	▶ Bombing in Saudi Arabia.
17 November 1997	▶ Massacre of 58 tourists at Luxor, Egypt.
August 1996	▶ Osama bin Laden issues first of three declarations of war against the USA.
23 February 1998	▶ Third and final declaration of war, calling on Muslims to attack all Americans.

It seems likely that other Islamic extremists were responsible for all these attacks. From 1998 on, however, al-Qaeda took the leading role in its self-declared war, launching a series of murderous assaults on US targets.

CROSS-REFERENCE
FAILED TERRORIST
PLOTS: PAGES
26–27, 36–37

An apartment block housing US personnel is bombed in Dhahran, Saudi Arabia, 26 June 1996.

Civilians too

'The ruling to kill the Americans and their allies, civilians and military, is an **individual duty for every Muslim** who can do it in any country in which it is possible to do it, in order to liberate the al-Aqsa mosque [in Jerusalem] and the holy mosque [Grand Mosque in Mecca] from their grip, and in order for their armies to move out of all the lands of Islam...'

From A Declaration of War by Osama bin Laden, Afghanistan, 23 February, 1998. Quoted in Rohan Gunaratna, Inside Al Qaeda (Hurst & Co, 2002).

African Embassy Attacks

On the morning of Friday, 7 August 1998, two young Saudi Arabians drove their truck into the US Embassy parking lot in Nairobi, Kenya. The men had been trained in one of al-Qaeda's Afghan camps and their truck was packed with explosives. The resulting blast seriously damaged the embassy and virtually destroyed the eight-storey secretarial college next door. It also killed 219 people. At almost the same moment a second team detonated another truck-load of explosives outside the US Embassy in Dar es Salaam, Tanzania. This killed 11 people. In both Nairobi and Dar es Salaam one of the bombers died with his victims. The other men were caught and soon confessed to their al-Qaeda connections.

Firemen search through the wreckage after the bombing of the US Embassy in Nairobi, Kenya, August 1998.

Nairobi eyewitness

The detonation punctuated the din of the street like a thunderclap. A few seconds later, we heard a deafening roar, as if a thousand thunderstorms had struck at once... The entire rear of the chancery was torn apart ... while an adjacent eight-story building, housing a secretarial college and other offices, collapsed on its occupants...'

The Nairobi Embassy bombing, as experienced by a US diplomat. Quoted on American Foreign Service website www.afsa.org/fsj/jun00/vandenbroucke.cfm

TIMELINE

TERRORIST ATTACKS AND US RESPONSES PRE-9/11 1998–2001

7 August 1998	▶ Bombings of US embassies in Kenya and Tanzania.
20 August 1998	▶ USA responds by launching strikes in Afghanistan and Sudan.
4 November 1998	▶ US Grand Jury charges Osama bin Laden with responsibility for the African embassy attacks.
14 November 1999	▶ UN resolution demands the surrender of Osama bin Laden.
December 1999	▶ Al-Qaeda bomb plot thwarted in Los Angeles.
12 October 2000	▶ Suicide attack on the destroyer USS *Cole* off the coast of Yemen.
29 May 2001	▶ Four al-Qaeda associates are convicted for their part in the African embassy bombings.
June 2001	▶ USA warns the Taliban government that it will be held responsible for attacks organized on its soil.

FIGHTING BACK

On 20 August the USA fired 75 Tomahawk cruise missiles at six camps in Afghanistan, killing 26. Bin Laden was not among them. On the same day a further seven missiles were fired at a factory in the Sudanese capital of Khartoum, which US intelligence claimed was producing chemical weapons. It later became clear that the factory produced medicines, and that several thousand people had died as a result of the subsequent shortages.

As anti-Western and anti-US feeling in the Muslim world reached new heights, more recruits travelled to al-Qaeda's training camps in Afghanistan. On 12 October 2000, two al-Qaeda-trained Yemenis sailed a small boat carrying explosives into the American destroyer USS *Cole*, which was lying at anchor off the Yemen coast. The explosion killed 17 US sailors.

The al-Shifa pharmaceutical factory in Khartoum, Sudan, after its wrongful destruction by US cruise missiles in August 1998.

MAJOR TERRORIST ATTACKS: PAGES 12–13, 30–31, 38–39, 40–41, 44–45

11

9/11

Between 8 and 9 a.m. on the morning of 11 September 2001, four passenger flights were hijacked in the northeastern USA. Two planes were flown into the twin towers of the World Trade Center in New York City, collapsing both and causing enormous loss of life. The third plane was crashed into the Pentagon headquarters of the US military, in Washington DC. The fourth failed to reach the hijackers' target. It was brought down in the Pennsylvania countryside after a violent struggle between the hijackers and passengers.

In less than two hours, 19 hijackers had killed around 3,000 people, and provided astonishing evidence of al-Qaeda's murderous reach. Unlike most countries, the US mainland had never suffered a large-scale assault from abroad, and most Americans were stunned by the scale, ferocity and unexpectedness of the attack. It felt like a war, but a war with whom? Before 9/11, few Americans had heard of al-Qaeda or Osama bin Laden.

THE US RESPONSE

On 12 September President George W. Bush provided the answer: the USA was at war with terrorism. Two days later, the US Congress passed the Use of Military Force Authorization, which gave President Bush the legal right to use 'all appropriate and necessary force' against this new enemy. On 21 September he insisted that all the world's governments should say which side they were on. 'Every nation in every region,' he said, 'now has a decision to make: either you are with us or you are with the terrorists.'

11 SEPTEMBER 2001

The destruction of New York City's World Trade Center on 11 September 2001.

9/11, BEFORE AND AFTER 2001

August 2001	▶ Osama bin Laden threatens 'unprecedented attacks' on the USA.
10 September 2001	▶ Bin Laden sets deadline for his deputies' return to Afghanistan.
11 September 2001	▶ Al-Qaeda launches its attacks on the USA.
13 September 2001	▶ Osama bin Laden is named as prime suspect by US Secretary of State Colin Powell.
14 September 2001	▶ US Congress authorizes President Bush to use whatever force he considers necessary to combat Islamic terrorism.
19 September 2001	▶ USA begins deploying forces in countries close to Afghanistan.
20 September 2001	▶ USA makes final demand to the Taliban government: give up Osama bin Laden or face invasion.

By this time the probable culprits had been identified. On 13 September US Secretary of State Colin Powell named Osama bin Laden as the prime suspect, and demanded that the Taliban government in Afghanistan hand him over.

CROSS-REFERENCE
TALIBAN: PAGES 16–17 ▶

Pentagon eyewitness

'As I was looking down at my desk, the plane caught my eye... I couldn't believe the pilot was flying so low. Then it dawned on me what was about to happen. **I watched in horror** as the plane flew at treetop level, banked slightly to the left, dragged its wing along the ground and slammed into the west wall of the Pentagon, exploding into a giant orange fireball.'

Steve Anderson, Director of Communications, USA TODAY. Quoted in www.whatreallyhappened.com

The Pentagon burns after an airliner is flown into it, 11 September 2001.

United Nations Security Council Resolution 1373

Although only the USA had been attacked on 9/11, an international response was necessary. Finding and defeating this global enemy would require a substantial increase in cooperation between the world's governments, intelligence services and financial institutions.

The early signs were good. On 28 September the United Nations Security Council unanimously adopted Resolution 1373, 'calling on states to work together urgently to prevent and suppress terrorist acts'. Governments were instructed to make fundraising for terrorism a criminal offence, and to freeze the accounts of individuals or groups suspected of involvement in terrorist activities. Governments were also prohibited from funding, arming or sheltering terrorist groups. Full and speedy cooperation was requested in international investigations.

Solidarity with the USA

'In this tragic moment, when words seem so inadequate to express the shock people feel, the first thing that comes to mind is this: **We are all Americans!**... Indeed, just as in the gravest moments of our own history, how can we not feel profound solidarity with those people, that country, the United States, to whom we are so close and to whom we owe our freedom, and therefore our solidarity?'

Editor Jean-Marie Colombani writing in *Le Monde* newspaper, France, 12 September, 2001.

28 SEPTEMBER 2001

Members of the United Nations Security Council observe a minute of silence for the victims of 9/11.

12 September 2001 ▶ NATO says attacks on USA are considered attacks on all 19 members of the alliance; United Nations Security Council Resolution 1368 condemns 9/11 attacks.

21 September 2001 ▶ President Bush says that if other nations are not 'with us', then they are 'against us'.

24 September 2001 ▶ Russia's President Putin pledges support for US war on terror.

Late September 2001 ▶ Pakistan's President Musharraf agrees to US use of Pakistani airbases for attack on Afghanistan.

28 September 2001 ▶ United Nations Security Council Resolution 1373 calls on all states to work together against terrorism.

INTERNATIONAL RESPONSE

Almost all governments expressed a willingness to join the war on terror, but some had reservations when it came to action. This was particularly true in the Muslim world. Most Muslim governments were keen to help, but many of their people supported or sympathized with Osama bin Laden and his goals. The Saudi government, for example, said it supported the war on terror, but refused to allow US planes the use of its airfields during the war in Afghanistan.

Other governments were motivated by different considerations. The war allowed them to brand opponents in their own countries as 'terrorists', and deal with them accordingly, without international criticism. Russia and Israel took particular advantage of the situation, arguing that their long-running conflicts with the Chechens and Palestinians had always been part of their war on terror.

US Secretary of State Colin Powell and Pakistan's President Pervez Musharraf, October 2001.

CROSS-REFERENCE CHECHENS: PAGES 32–33 ▶

'Operation Enduring Freedom'

After 9/11 the al-Qaeda leaders suspected of financing and planning the attacks remained in Afghanistan, and the Taliban government showed no sign of handing them over. A military operation would be needed to remove them. By the end of September 2001, US special forces were operating inside Afghanistan, and a major air assault was imminent. Despite doubts arising over these actions, there were few protests from other governments. Almost everyone agreed that al-Qaeda had to be stopped, and that this was the quickest method.

A COSTLY OPERATION

On 7 October 'Operation Enduring Freedom' began. US planes and British aircraft carriers in the Arabian Gulf began bombing Taliban and al-Qaeda targets. The original intention was to move swiftly from bombing to ground operations by special forces, but the first ground operation proved a disaster, and the bombings were intensified. Taliban resistance was broken, but at a great cost: more civilians died during the bombings than had died in the 9/11 attacks.

Most of the ground-fighting was done by the Afghans of the Northern Alliance, a loose grouping of long-term opponents of the Taliban. By early December they had captured three major Afghan cities, including the country's capital, Kabul. Meanwhile, in Germany powerful Afghans were busy choosing a new interim (temporary) government to rule their country.

A US F-14 fighter-bomber takes off from an aircraft carrier in the Indian Ocean during 'Operation Enduring Freedom', October 2001.

CROSS-REFERENCE
TALIBAN: PAGES
12–13

TIMELINE	**INVASION OF AFGHANISTAN 2001**

AL-QAEDA'S LEADERS

One al-Qaeda leader, the military commander Mohammed Atef, had been killed in a US bombing raid, but there was no sign of the others. Following reports that they were hiding in the Tora Bora cave complex that area was bombed and searched, but to no avail. Al-Qaeda had lost its place of safety in Afghanistan, but most of its leaders remained at large.

20 September 2001 ▶ USA makes final demand to the Taliban government: give up Osama bin Laden or face invasion.

7 October 2001 ▶ Air strikes against Afghanistan begin.

19 October 2001 ▶ USA begins ground operations in Afghanistan.

9 November 2001 ▶ Northern Alliance capture Kabul.

16 November 2001 ▶ Al-Qaeda military commander Mohammed Atef killed by US air strike.

25 November 2001 ▶ Afghan representatives meet in Germany to organize post-Taliban government.

6 December 2001 ▶ Northern Alliance capture Taliban's home city of Kandahar.

22 December 2001 ▶ Hamid Karzai sworn in as interim Afghan prime minister.

Mohammad Doud, one of the Northern Alliance commanders, answers journalist's questions during 'Operation Enduring Freedom'.

The Taliban

The Taliban movement began in the early 1990s. Young men who had attended religious colleges in neighbouring Pakistan were armed and funded by the Pakistani government, and encouraged to end the chaos which had engulfed Afghanistan since the defeat of the Communist government there in 1989. By 1996 the Taliban controlled most of the country. They set up a central government in Kabul, and introduced an unusually strict interpretation of Islamic religious laws. Music, for example, was completely banned, and women virtually imprisoned in their homes.

USA PATRIOT Act

Members of a Biological Incident Response Force check for anthrax in a US government building.

The threat of further terrorist attacks convinced the governments of the developed countries that they needed more powers to protect themselves and their citizens. In October 2001, the US Congress passed the Uniting and Strengthening America by Providing Appropriate Tools Required to Intercept and Obstruct Terrorism Act (USA PATRIOT Act). This defined terrorism as acts of violence that 'appear to be intended to influence the policy of government by intimidation or coercion'. It gave the authorities power to search the computers and financial and medical records of anyone suspected of involvement in terrorist activities. Such suspects could be arrested without due process (normal legal rights), be held without trial and have their property seized.

REACTIONS IN THE USA

The mainstream American media, along with most Americans, supported such measures. On 12 September one

NBC announcer argued that he and his fellow-citizens might have to sacrifice 'some of the freedoms we have'. A poll taken by the ABC network found that two-thirds of Americans were indeed prepared to give up some of their civil liberties for a more secure society. If the measures contained in the USA PATRIOT Act really were eroding civil liberties, then most

Total Information Awareness

The US Department of Defense introduced its new Total Information Awareness system in November 2002. This could search the global computer network for any information that might prove helpful in the war on terror. It could access credit card records, passport applications and arrest records. It could trace the buyers of any goods and services – such as airline tickets, guns and dangerous chemicals – for which sellers were obliged to keep records.

20 September 2001	▶ US Department of Homeland Security is set up.
26 October 2001	▶ USA PATRIOT Act is passed.
19 November 2001	▶ UK Anti-Terrorism, Crime and Security Act is passed.
18 June 2002	▶ US Homeland Security Act is passed.
November 2002	▶ US Department of Defense introduces Total Information Awareness system for gathering intelligence.
7 February 2003	▶ Details of a second PATRIOT Act are leaked to the media. The Act is much criticized and is withdrawn.
November 2005	▶ British government fails to win parliamentary support for an extension of the time terror suspects can be held without charge to 90 days.

Americans believed the sacrifice was a worthwhile one. Those who disapproved of the Act claimed that its definition of terrorism would include American heroes like George Washington and Martin Luther King. They also believed that the new measures weakened personal and legal rights that Americans had always taken for granted.

REACTIONS IN EUROPE

Similar arguments began in the UK and other European countries in the aftermath of 9/11. As there is no clear answer to the basic question 'How far are governments justified in limiting individual liberties for the security of all?', the arguments cannot easily be resolved.

CROSS-REFERENCE NEW POWERS FOR US GOVERNMENT: PAGES 20–21

US Attorney-General John Ashcroft, defending new anti-terrorism measures before a Senate committee, December 2001.

First Detainees Arrive at Guantánamo

11 JANUARY 2002

On 11 January 2002 the US military delivered the first batch of war-on-terror prisoners to Camp X-Ray, a newly built prison complex inside the US naval base at Cuba's Guantánamo Bay. Most of these men were captured in Afghanistan, but later batches included captives from all over the world. By mid-2003 Camp X-Ray housed over 700 prisoners from over 40 countries.

ENEMY COMBATANTS

The US administration insisted that the Guantánamo detainees were not prisoners of war (POWs), as defined by the Geneva Convention (rules governing the rights of individuals during conflict and war). They therefore refused these captives the rights and status of POWs. Administration officials pointed to Article 4 of the Convention, which defines POWs as regular soldiers, guerrillas or members of militias. They claimed that the detainees – all alleged members of Al-Qaeda or the Taliban – had been none of these. Instead, they created a new category for them: enemy combatants.

The US government has been criticized for its treatment of prisoners at Guantánamo Bay. Classifying them as enemy combatants rather than POWs allowed the government to hold them

A new prisoner is escorted into Camp X-Ray detention centre, Guantánamo Bay, February 2002.

Guantánamo eyewitness

'There was another interrogation room, on which they had written "Hell" in Arabic. If you didn't cooperate, you went there... There were enormous speakers on the walls and projectors on the ceiling. They bound the detainees and put on the music full blast, often techno music. The spotlights flashed very strong, very fast bursts of white light... **you feel like your brain is going to dissolve.** Some people stayed there two days.'

A description of Guantánamo by former detainee Mourad Benchellali. Quoted in *Libération*, 20 February 2006.

CROSS-REFERENCE
NEW POWERS FOR
US GOVERNMENT:
PAGES 18–19

TIMELINE

GUANTÁNAMO 2002–2006

11 January 2002 ▶ First detainees arrive at Guantánamo Bay.

July 2003 ▶ By now around 680 detainees from 42 countries are incarcerated at Guantánamo.

23 July 2003 ▶ Major General Geoffrey Miller claims that three-quarters of the detainees have confessed to some involvement in terrorism.

30 November 2004 ▶ *New York Times* prints allegations of torture at Guantánamo.

19 November 2005 ▶ UN visit is cancelled when USA refuses to allow private meetings between UN delegates and detainees.

13 June 2006 ▶ European Parliament urges USA to close Camp X-Ray.

19 June 2006 ▶ US Supreme Court rules that detainees are entitled to protection under the Geneva Convention.

for long periods without trial. There have also been allegations of ill-treatment.

SUPREME COURT JUDGEMENTS

According to the US administration, Guantánamo lay outside the jurisdiction of the US legal system. However, in June 2004 the US Supreme Court decided otherwise. Two years later, in June 2006, the Supreme Court went further, ruling that the detainees were entitled to the protection of the Geneva Convention. The following month, the US Department of Defense agreed to abide by this judgement.

By November 2006, 340 of the 775 detainees at Guantánamo had been released and a further 180 were soon to be released or to face trial.

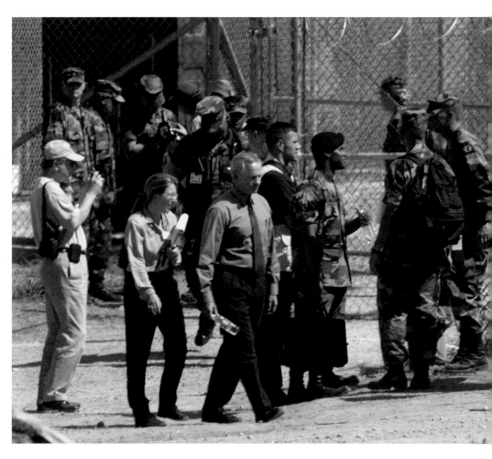

Members of a US government delegation visit Camp X-Ray, January 2002.

'Axis of Evil' Speech

On 29 January 2002 President Bush delivered his annual State of the Union address to the US Congress. The elimination of individual terrorists and terrorist groups was one goal, he said, but there was another. The USA's second goal was to 'prevent regimes that sponsor terror from threatening America or our friends and allies with weapons of mass destruction…' He named three governments – those of North Korea, Iran and Iraq. 'States like these, and their terrorist allies, constitute an axis of evil, arming to threaten the peace of the world.'

This speech proved very controversial. The three states he cited were thought to be developing weapons of mass destruction, but they had no obvious links with al-Qaeda, and were unlikely to have any in the future. None had any sympathy for the Sunni Muslim extremism that al-Qaeda represented.

WIDENING THE WAR

So why did President Bush seek to widen the war on terror to include these regimes? There were several possible reasons. He may have genuinely believed that they would hand over weapons of mass destruction to terrorists. Another reason was that the war on terror could be used as part of a wider strategy to bring a new order to the oil-rich Middle East and other parts of the world identified as a potential threat. The aim was to stabilize those

29 JANUARY 2002

Workers in the Middle East fill an oil tanker with oil – the region's most sought-after commodity.

regions in the interests of the USA and its allies. Neo-conservatives in the administration had long argued for this strategy. Most observers believe that safeguarding oil supplies is central to US policy in the Middle East.

FOCUSING ON IRAQ

The USA's growing determination to confront Iraq would lead, 14 months later, to the invasion of that country. Most of the USA's allies disliked this new policy. They wanted to pursue the original war on terror. The Bush administration, they believed, had taken its eye off the ball.

CROSS-REFERENCE
PRESIDENT GEORGE W. BUSH: PAGES 28–29, 44–45
WAR IN IRAQ: PAGES 34–35, 38–39

US Secretary of Defense Donald Rumsfeld at a Pentagon press briefing, September 2002.

The Project for a New American Century

The Project for a New American Century was set up by American neo-conservatives in 1997. In 1998 the group sent an open letter to President Clinton, suggesting that he remove the Iraqi leader Saddam Hussein from power as a first step towards rearranging the Middle East along more pro-US lines. Many who signed the letter – future Defense Secretary Donald Rumsfeld, for example – held high office in the first George W. Bush administration, which invaded Iraq in 2003.

Capture of Abu Zubaydah

28 MARCH 2002

In late March 2002 US intelligence traced two phone calls from Abu Zubaydah, one of the men on their al-Qaeda 'most-wanted' list. It led them to a house in the Pakistani town of Faisalabad. On 28 March US and Pakistani security forces stormed the building and made the arrest. News of the successful operation was quickly broadcast. Abu Zubaydah was described as al-Qaeda's chief recruiter and top military strategist. His capture was clearly an important victory in the war on terror.

Or was it? Just how important were the leaders of al-Qaeda in early 2002? If al-Qaeda operated like a global army, with a few generals passing down instructions and orders to thousands of obedient privates, then the generals were clearly important. But al-Qaeda did not operate in that way.

AL-QAEDA AND 9/11

Before 9/11, the leading members of al-Qaeda were based in Afghanistan, enjoying the hospitality of the Taliban government. They offered terrorist training to individuals and groups who shared their ideas and gave money and planning advice to those who thought up promising projects. They also occasionally suggested, financed and organized operations of their own.

After 9/11, when most of these leaders were on the run, their links with the outside world were much fewer. Al-Qaeda had become less important as an organization, but more important as an idea and an inspiration.

Before 9/11 several thousand men had been trained in Afghanistan. Most had gone back to their home countries or gone to fight in one of the conflicts involving Muslims. Inspired by 9/11, many of them recruited others, formed groups and launched their own attacks. When such groups claimed links to al-Qaeda, they were talking about shared ideas, not continuing contact.

One of 22 posters depicting the FBI's 'Most Wanted Terrorists'.

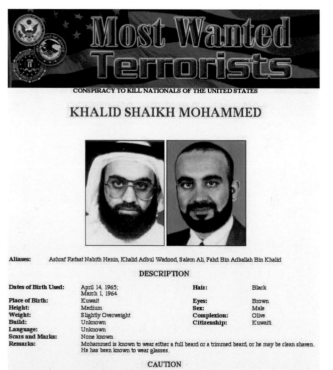

A video star

Since 9/11 Osama bin Laden has been a hunted man. It seems unlikely that he has been able to play any practical part in the war that he declared in 1998, but regular appearances on video and audiotape have kept him in the public eye. These appearances, which are given global coverage by the al-Jazeera Arab TV channel, offer proof of his survival, both taunting his enemies and inspiring his allies.

CROSS-REFERENCE
HUNT FOR AL-QAEDA:
PAGES 44–45

Al-Qaeda leader Osama bin Laden poses with a weapon early in 2001.

Arrest of the 'Dirty Bomber'

Jose Padilla was born in Brooklyn, New York City, of Puerto Rican parents. In the 1990s he converted to Islam, changed his name to Abdullah al-Muhajir, and travelled to Afghanistan with the intention of making contact with other Islamic extremists. In 2001 he was sent to Lahore for training in the making of a radioactive 'dirty bomb'. It seems likely that al-Qaeda adopted him because his US passport allowed him easy entrance to the USA.

Al-Muhajir was arrested on arrival at Chicago's O'Hare Airport on 8 May 2002. The US authorities claimed that the arrest was a wonderful example of inter-agency cooperation and efficient intelligence-gathering. The impression was given that a major plot had been foiled. In reality, al-Muhajir was probably on a fact-finding mission. He had no 'dirty bomb' with him, and there was no suggestion that he or al-Qaeda had the material with which to make one.

FEAR OF MASS DESTRUCTION

Al-Muhajir presented no immediate danger, but the fear that terrorists might acquire and use weapons of mass destruction remained all too real.

In the weeks following 9/11 five people had died as a result of handling letters containing anthrax spores, and the culprits had not been

Abdullah al-Muhajir, the 'Dirty Bomber'.

caught. That was bad enough, but governments feared something much worse – that terrorists would succeed in using chemical, biological or nuclear weapons in a major city, causing thousands, or even millions, of deaths. Preventing this from happening had become a crucial part of the war on terror.

THE CASE OF DHIREN BAROT

In August 2004 Dhiren Barot, a British citizen of Indian origin, was arrested in north London and charged with planning chemical or radioactive attacks against unnamed UK targets. A few months later the US authorities charged him with planning attacks on

23 December 2001 ▶ The 'Shoe Bomber' is overpowered on a transatlantic flight.

8 May 2002 ▶ The alleged 'Dirty Bomber' is arrested in Chicago.

12–13 May 2002 ▶ Three Saudi Arabian suicide bombers are arrested in Morocco before their planned assault on US and UK warships

5 January 2003 ▶ Police raiding a flat in north London claim to have found traces of the deadly poison ricin. They are later found to be wrong.

12 August 2003 ▶ Missile-importer Hemant Lakhani is arrested during a 'sting operation' set up by US, British and Russian intelligence.

August 2004 ▶ Dhiren Barot is arrested and pleads guilty to planning chemical and radioactive attacks on UK and US targets.

10 August 2006 ▶ UK Home Secretary John Reid announces that a plot to blow up several transatlantic airliners has been foiled by British and Pakistani intelligence.

Richard Reid, the 'Shoe Bomber', under arrest in Boston, December 2001.

The 'Shoe Bomber'

Richard Reid grew up in London and soon drifted into crime. During a spell in prison he converted to Islam, and after his release he found himself drawn to its most extreme interpretations.

On 22 December 2001 Reid boarded a Miami-bound plane in Paris with shoes containing explosive devices. He was spotted attempting to light a fuse in mid-air and was overpowered by his fellow-passengers. The plane was diverted to Boston, USA, and he was arrested on arrival.

major financial institutions, including the Stock Exchange in New York City and the World Bank headquarters in Washington DC. On 7 November 2006, after pleading guilty to these charges, Barot was sentenced to life imprisonment. As it turned out, experts believed that the bombs he had intend to use were unlikely to have killed anyone.

CROSS-REFERENCE
FAILED TERRORIST
PLOTS: PAGES
36–37
WEAPONS OF MASS
DESTRUCTION:
PAGES 34–35,
36–37

Bush Doctrine

On 1 June 2002 President Bush used a speech at the USA's West Point Military Academy to announce a new strategy for the war on terror. In the past, he said, the USA had 'relied on the Cold War doctrines of deterrence and containment'. He was referring to the years of rivalry between the USA and the Soviet Union following the Second World War. During that period the USA had relied on its possession of nuclear weapons and the threat of destruction which they presented in order to deter the Soviet Union from launching a first strike.

This reliance on Cold War doctrines, he argued, had to change. Terrorism was a new and very different enemy. Deterrence meant 'nothing against shadowy terrorist networks with no nation or citizens to defend'. Containment (preventing the spread of the enemy's power) was not possible 'when unbalanced dictators with weapons of mass destruction can deliver those weapons on missiles or secretly provide them to terrorist allies'. If the USA was to defeat terrorism, it had to be prepared to take pre-emptive action – that is, to strike first.

CRITICISM OF THE POLICY

This new policy – which soon became known as the Bush Doctrine – was highly controversial. Critics agreed that a new approach was needed to counter the terrorist threat, but disagreed with this one. Pre-emptive

President George W. Bush speaking at West Point Military Academy, 1 June 2002.

Full spectrum dominance

In May 2000 the US Department of Defense issued *Joint Vision 2020*, an examination of the military challenges facing the US over the next two decades. According to the document, the aim of US military policy should be 'full spectrum dominance', by which it meant the ability to control any situation and defeat any enemy that the country might face, with or without allied help.

TIMELINE

THE BUSH DOCTRINE 1991–2003

1991–92 ▶ Under-Secretary of Defense for Policy Paul Wolfowitz co-writes *Defense Planning Guidance*, a blueprint for future US policy which recommends pre-emptive US strikes.

January 2001 ▶ Wolfowitz is appointed Deputy Defense Secretary in the first George W. Bush administration.

1 June 2002 ▶ President George W. Bush announces the 'Bush Doctrine' at the West Point Military Academy.

20 September 2002 ▶ *The National Security Strategy of the United States of America* is published.

20 March 2003 ▶ The invasion of Iraq puts the Bush Doctrine into practice.

action, they pointed out, is forbidden by the United Nations Charter. The Charter permits military action in self-defence in only two circumstances – when a national border has been crossed by an invading country, or following a decision of the United Nations Security Council. When supporters of the US administration argued that the USA had the right to invade and disarm other states before they could use weapons of mass destruction, opponents countered that other states could invade the USA with exactly the same intention.

REAFFIRMATION

In September 2002 the Bush administration produced a document called *The National Security Strategy of the United States of America*. This reaffirmed the Bush Doctrine. Western-style democracy, it claimed, was the 'single surviving model of human progress', and the USA was pledged to defend it. The war on terror had become a war for democracy.

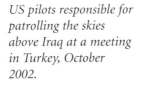

CROSS-REFERENCE PRESIDENT GEORGE W. BUSH, PAGES 22–23, 44–45

US pilots responsible for patrolling the skies above Iraq at a meeting in Turkey, October 2002.

Bali Bombing

On the evening of Saturday 12 October 2002 several hundred young Westerners – most of them Australians – were packed into the popular Sari nightclub on Bali's famous Kuta Beach. Soon after 11 p.m. a van full of explosives was detonated just outside the club. Around 200 people were killed by the blast and fires that followed, and many more were injured. The bombers, it was eventually discovered, were Indonesian Muslims with only faint links to al-Qaeda.

WHY INDONESIA?

Why had Indonesian Muslims joined the terrorist side in the global war on terror? Indonesia is not a Middle Eastern country, but it does have a large Muslim majority. Many Indonesian Muslims, like many Middle Eastern Muslims, blamed the West for their undemocratic governments and harsh working conditions, and resented what they perceived as a lack of respect for Islam. The vast majority expressed their disaffection in non-violent ways. A few, inspired by al-Qaeda's dramatic campaign, turned to terror.

Bali eyewitness

'I was dancing to Eminem, enjoying the flow, when I heard the first bang. Many people stood still, and then there was a second. **It was an incredible force of wind and heat.** Somehow I managed to climb out through the roof. I was in the street in a complete daze, yelling out my boyfriend's name, but I had a strong feeling that he was dead.'

The words of Hanabeth Luke, whose boyfriend Mark died in the Sari nightclub.

Bali's Kuta Beach resort after the nightclub bombing of 12 October 2002.

WHY THE SARI NIGHTCLUB?

The attack on the Sari nightclub was supposed to strike fear into Western tourists everywhere, and to deter them from visiting Muslim countries. The Sari nightclub, by either luck or design, provided the terrorists with one potent symbol of Western arrogance: local people were not allowed in. The aftermath of the blast provided another: injured Westerners received better medical treatment than injured locals.

FITTING THE PATTERN

The Bali bombing was only one in a series of similar outrages between April 2002 and the end of 2003. Major terrorist attacks took place in Tunisia, Kenya, Turkey, Saudi Arabia and Morocco. Minor attacks took place in many other countries. Almost every incident revealed the same pattern: a group of young men, inspired but not organized by al-Qaeda, targeting Western tourists or Western interests in a Muslim town or country.

CROSS-REFERENCE
MAJOR TERRORIST ATTACKS: PAGES 10–11, 12–13, 38–39, 40–41, 44–45

Amrozi bin Haji Nurhasyim, found guilty of involvement in the Bali bombings, is brought to court in August 2003. He was sentenced to death.

Moscow Theatre Siege Begins

The Moscow theatre siege of October 2002 was one of many attacks launched by Chechen terrorists since the arrival of the new Russian government in 1990. Muslims from the small mountain region of Chechnya number over a million, and have been waging wars for their independence since the eighteenth century. In the 1990s some Chechen groups adopted the tactics of terrorism. These groups included Chechens trained in Afghanistan and Arab volunteers, who came to help the Chechens once the war in Afghanistan had ended.

THE SIEGE

The Moscow theatre siege began on the evening of 23 October 2002, when 42 Chechen rebels – half of them women – entered the House of Culture theatre in Moscow. They took the entire audience of over 900 people hostage, and demanded the withdrawal of Russian troops from Chechnya. The siege ended early on 26 October, when Soviet special forces pumped disabling gas into the theatre and stormed in. All the rebels were killed, many executed on the spot. At least 120 hostages were killed, most of them by the gas. The Russian

Russian special forces outside the theatre seized by Chechen terrorists, October 2002.

TIMELINE

CROSS-REFERENCE
CHECHENS: PAGES
14–15

CHECHNYA 1991–2004

October 1991 ▶	Chechen declaration of independence follows break-up of Soviet Union. It is not recognized by Russia or the international community.
1994–96 ▶	First Chechen War ends in victory for Chechens after a great loss of Chechen lives.
1999–2000 ▶	Second Chechen War ends in Russian reoccupation.
23 October 2002 ▶	Moscow theatre siege is launched by Chechen terrorists. It ends on 26 October.
6 February 2004 ▶	Chechen terrorists bomb Moscow metro, killing 42 and injuring 250.
27 August 2004 ▶	Two airliners are brought down by Chechen terrorists.
1 September 2004 ▶	Beslan school siege is launched. It ends on 3 September.

government, while regretting the loss of innocent life, declared its action a triumph in the war on terror.

NEW JUSTIFICATION

Before 9/11 Western governments had frequently criticized the brutal behaviour of the Russian armed forces in Chechnya. Since 9/11 the Russian government has consistently used the war on terror to justify the same sort of behaviour, and any criticism of their actions has been suppressed.

Those Chechen groups who favour terrorism have made things easier for the Russians and their allies. Terrorist operations such as the Beslan school siege of September 2004 (see the box below) reinforce the international determination to outlaw terrorism.

Flowers and water bottles left in memory of those who died in the Beslan school siege, September 2004.

The Beslan school siege

A major terrorist outrage involving the Chechens was the Beslan school siege of September 2004. Thirty-two Chechens took over the school (in North Ossetia, which borders Chechnya) and seized 1,200 children and adults hostage. Negotiations failed, and, after shooting broke out on the third day, the authorities stormed the school. Of the 344 people killed, 186 were children.

Invasion of Iraq

Ever since Iraq's defeat in the 1991 Gulf War there had been fears that Saddam Hussein's government was trying to build nuclear, chemical and biological weapons of mass destruction. After 9/11, the Western powers feared that Iraq might hand these weapons over to terrorists. In order, they said, to prevent this happening, the USA and UK led an invasion of Iraq on 20 March 2003. Hussein was overthrown, and eventually captured, tried and executed. Western troops remained in the country.

NEW JUSTIFICATION

No link was found between Hussein's government and al-Qaeda. No weapons of mass destruction were discovered. The invasion, which had originally been justified as part of the war on terror, was now explained as a war for democracy. Many critics of the war argued that the West was simply using the war on terror to destroy an old enemy, bolster its strategic position and seize control of Iraq's important oil reserves.

RESISTANCE ON THE GROUND

In Iraq there was resistance to the occupation from the beginning. Several groups were involved. Aside from remnants of Saddam's regime, there were rival Muslim factions – Sunni Muslims who feared a Shia majority government, and Shias opposed to any foreign presence in Iraq. They were soon joined by

volunteers from outside Iraq – Islamic extremists who wanted to fight Westerners.

Before the invasion Iraq played no part in the war on terror, but by the end of 2003 it had become one of that war's major battlegrounds.

US soldiers en route to Iraq, 27 March 2003.

TIMELINE

INVASION AND OCCUPATION OF IRAQ 2002–2006

29 January 2002	President Bush says that Iraq is part of an 'Axis of Evil'.
November 2002	Under pressure, Iraq allows UN weapons inspectors back into the country.
February 2003	USA and UK fail to win UN support for immediate military action.
20 March 2003	Invasion of Iraq begins.
9 April 2003	Baghdad falls to US forces.
13 December 2003	Saddam Hussein is captured.
7 June 2006	Abu Musab al-Zarqawi, leader of al-Qaeda in Iraq, is killed by a US air strike.
June–July 2006	Around 6,000 Iraqis are killed. Most of the violence occurs between competing Islamic groups.
30 December 2006	After a lengthy trial, Saddam Hussein is executed in Iraq.

An oil pipeline set ablaze by Iraqi insurgents, December 2005.

CONSEQUENCES

The consequences for the wider war on terror were enormous. Disagreements over the invasion had seriously weakened the international unity which marked the post-9/11 period. Worse still, the behaviour of some of the occupying forces – including prisoner abuse and civilian massacres – convinced many Muslims that Osama bin Laden was right: the West really was targeting them and their religion.

**CROSS-REFERENCE
WAR IN IRAQ:
PAGES 22–23,
38–39
WEAPONS OF MASS
DESTRUCTION:
PAGES 26–27,
36–37**

Losing the focus?

'I am deeply concerned that the policy we are presently following with respect to Iraq has the potential to seriously damage our ability to win the war against terrorism and to weaken our ability to lead the world in this new century...'

From a speech given by former Vice-President Al Gore, 23 September 2002.

Missile Sting

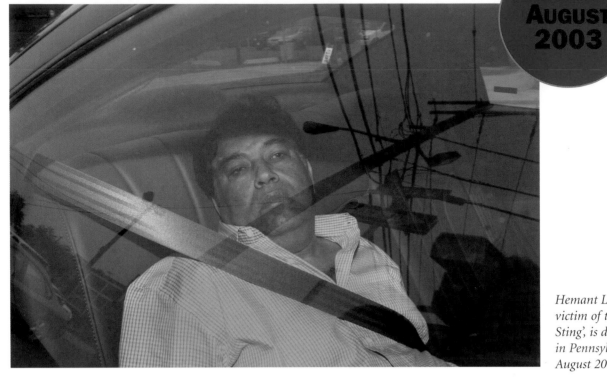

12 AUGUST 2003

Hemant Lakhani, victim of the 'Missile Sting', is driven to court in Pennsylvania, USA, August 2003.

The terrorist group who bombed the Paradise Hotel in Mombasa, Kenya, on 28 November 2002 also fired two SA-7 surface-to-air missiles at an Israeli airliner departing the city airport. They missed, but the possibility of a successful missile attack on a crowded airliner continued to worry intelligence services.

CATCHING LAKHANI

In March 2003 agents of the Russian security police (FSB) became aware that an Indian-born British arms dealer named Hemant Lakhani was in St Petersburg to buy weapons. The British and US intelligence services (MI5 and FBI) were informed, and while MI5 looked into Lakhani's background, an FBI agent was sent to join the surveillance team in the Russian capital.

The Russians manufactured a false (non-working) version of their Igla missile, sold it to the unsuspecting Lakhani, and waited to see what would happen.

Biological scares

On 5 October 2001 a newspaper employee in Florida was sent an envelope containing deadly anthrax spores. He and four subsequent victims died. Several politicians were sent similar doses of the lethal bacteria, but managed to avoid any contact with it. The sender or senders were never traced.

In January 2003 British police claimed that they had found traces of the deadly poison ricin. The media was suddenly full of scare stories, and the British government was eager to stress the seriousness of the threat. It was, however, all a mistake. There had been no ricin.

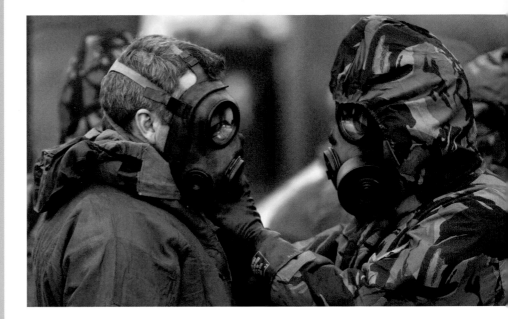

British police officers protect themselves against possible chemical weapons before searching a suspected terrorist's home, January 2003.

The arms dealer shipped the missile by boat to Baltimore, and flew back to the US under the watchful eye of the FBI agent. There was no doubt that Lakhani intended selling the Igla to Islamic terrorists – he was heard calling Osama bin Laden a 'hero' and expressing his hatred of Americans. When he went to pick up the shipment – which was marked 'medical supplies' – Lakhani was arrested. Colleagues were also taken into custody, and all of the arms dealer's contacts thoroughly investigated.

INTERNATIONAL CO-OPERATION

The whole operation was made possible by an agreement reached at that year's G8 summit – an annual meeting between eight of the world's wealthiest nations: the USA, Japan, Germany, France, the UK, Italy, Canada and Russia. They agreed to keep a better watch on the world's missiles. The US, British and Russian intelligence services had never worked so closely together.

CROSS-REFERENCE WEAPONS OF MASS DESTRUCTION: PAGES 26–27, 34–35 FAILED TERRORIST PLOTS: PAGES 8–9, 26–27

Madrid Bombings

11 MARCH 2004

Although the USA supplied well over 90 per cent of the occupation forces in Iraq, several other countries contributed small contingents. Spain had been a prominent supporter of the US-led invasion in 2003, and by the end of that year around 1,300 Spanish troops were deployed in Iraq. A Spanish general election was due on 14 March 2004, and the opposition Socialist Party was committed to withdrawing those troops.

EVENTS IN MADRID

On the morning of 11 March bombs were exploded on four commuter trains in the Spanish capital Madrid. The explosions killed 191 people and wounded over 2,000. On the following day over 11 million people filled the streets of Spain's towns and cities with a series of peaceful protests against the attacks. Before the bombings it was widely expected that the weekend's general election would be won by the ruling People's Party, but the Socialist Party had a surprise victory. It seemed highly probable that the bombings – and the fear of more attacks – had made the difference.

The newly elected Socialist government was in an impossible position. If it failed to bring the troops home from Iraq, it would be breaking its promise to the Spanish electorate. If the troops were brought back to Spain, then the terrorists

Forensic experts examine victims of the Madrid train bombings, 11 March 2004.

CROSS-REFERENCE
WAR IN IRAQ:
PAGES 22–23,
34–35

TIMELINE

MADRID BOMBINGS, BEFORE AND AFTER 2003–2004

August 2003 ▶ Spain sends combat troops to Iraq.

February–March 2004 ▶ In the run-up to the general election, the opposition Socialist Party promises to withdraw Spanish troops from Iraq.

11 March 2004 ▶ Madrid bombings.

12 March 2004 ▶ The Spanish government suggests that the Basque separatist group ETA was responsible for the bombings.

13 March 2004 ▶ The Socialist Party wins the election, and reaffirms that it will withdraw Spanish troops from Iraq.

15 April 2004 ▶ Osama bin Laden offers a truce to any European country 'which commits itself to not attacking Muslims'.

May 2004 ▶ Last Spanish troops leave Iraq.

would be able to claim that their bombings had influenced both a European election and the situation in Iraq. The troops were brought home.

A VICTORY FOR BIN LADEN?

A few weeks later, on 15 April, Osama bin Laden tried to build on this apparent victory. In an audiotape sent to Arab broadcasters he offered a truce to Europeans. If their countries stopped 'attacking Muslims or interfering in their affairs', then al-Qaeda would not mount operations against them. Withdraw like the Spanish, he seemed to be saying, and your capital will avoid the fate of Madrid.

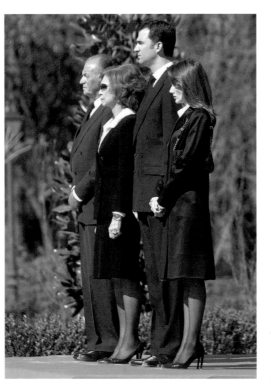

The Spanish royal family at the opening of the 'Forest of the Departed' memorial garden, 11 March 2005.

Forest of the Departed

On the first anniversary of the Madrid bombings a memorial garden was opened near Atocha Station in the centre of the Spanish capital. *Bosque de los Ausentes* ('Forest of the Departed') contains 192 olive and cypress trees, one for each victim and one for the special agent who was killed in the subsequent police operation.

London Bombings

The London bus destroyed by one of four suicide bombers, 7 July 2005.

The Madrid bombers were almost certainly North African Muslims from Morocco and Tunisia. The London bombers were not foreigners – they were British Muslims. At around 8.30 a.m. on 7 July (7/7) the four young men arrived at Kings Cross Thameslink station and split up. Around 20 minutes later three of them detonated the explosives they were carrying on separate underground trains. The fourth bomber, for reasons that remain unclear, exploded his bomb on a London bus almost an hour later. A total of 56 people were killed and around 700 injured.

THE BOMBERS

At least two of the four London bombers had visited Pakistan, where they probably had meetings with

London eyewitness

'We travelled out into the tunnel and not long after we set out all I saw was yellow light and what appeared to be silver lines in front of my eyes – which turned out to be the glass.... Our carriage was smoke-filled, there was lots of dust, there was lots of panic. **We could hear the screams** from the carriage where the bomb had gone off – they were trapped in twisted metal.'

The words of eyewitness Michael Henning, BBC News, Friday 8 July.

CROSS-REFERENCE
SUICIDE BOMBINGS:
PAGES 6–7,
42–43

TIMELINE	THE UK AND THE WAR ON TERROR 2001–2006
19 November 2001	▸ UK Anti-Terrorism, Crime and Security Act.
24 September 2002	▸ British government argues that Iraqi weapons of mass destruction pose a significant threat to the UK.
January– February 2003	▸ British government persuades the US government to take the problem of Iraq to the UN.
5 January 2003	▸ Alleged discovery of the deadly poison ricin in a London flat sparks a major scare.
20 March 2003	▸ Despite huge public protests, the UK joins the USA in the invasion of Iraq.
7 July 2005	▸ The London bombings.
21 July 2005	▸ Attempted bombing attacks in London fail.
10 August 2006	▸ British Home Secretary announces that a plot to blow up 12 flights from UK airports has been thwarted.

members of al-Qaeda. There is nothing to suggest that they received any training in bomb-making, however, or that they were asked to carry out a particular operation. It seems likely that they found the technical information they needed on the internet, and dreamt up the operation themselves. Their anger at British foreign policy in the Middle East and their hatred for the country and culture in which they had grown up was all the motivation they needed to launch their attacks.

THE ENEMY WITHIN

The fact that four British-born young men had carried out the attack was both shocking and significant. After 7/7 it became clear that, for Britain at least, fighting the war on terror was no longer simply a matter of keeping enemies out. The 'enemy' was already inside the walls. The challenge for the British authorities was to prevent more young Muslims from feeling such hatred for their own country.

Three of the 7/7 suicide bombers caught on CCTV at Luton station, a week before the attacks.

Hamas Election Victory

25 JANUARY 2006

On 25 January 2006, elections in the Israeli-occupied Palestinian territories were won by the Hamas organization. Hamas does not recognize the State of Israel. Created in 1987, Hamas is listed as a terrorist organization by the USA, European Union and others. It has used terrorist tactics – particularly suicide bombings – but it has also attacked military targets.

WHY HAMAS?

There were two principal reasons for the Hamas victory. Unlike the previous ruling party, Fatah – which was considered both dishonest and incompetent by many Palestinians – Hamas was trusted. More importantly, perhaps, Fatah had failed to make progress towards ending the Israeli occupation of the West Bank and Gaza Strip. The Israeli withdrawal of 7,000 settlers from Gaza in 2005 was not considered significant by most Palestinians. Israeli military incursions (raids) had continued, and over 300,000 settlers remained in the West Bank. By voting for Hamas, a majority of Palestinians showed their desire for a government that effectively opposed the occupation, even if it also supported terrorism.

The Hamas victory clearly had implications for the war on terror. President Bush had stated that the war on terror was also a war for

Hamas supporters celebrate their victory in the Palestinian elections of January 2006.

The UN view

'Any group that wishes to participate in the democratic process **should ultimately disarm**, because to carry weapons and participate in a democratic process and sit in parliament, there is a fundamental contradiction and I'm sure they (Hamas) are thinking about that too.'

Kofi Annan, the UN Secretary-General, speaking after Hamas' victory in the Palestinian elections of January 2006.

THE GROWTH OF HAMAS
TIMELINE 1987–2006

1987 ▶ Hamas is founded.

1992 ▶ Hamas' military wing – the *Izz ad-Din al-Qassam* – is formed.

16 April 1993 ▶ First Hamas suicide bombing in Israel, at Mehola Junction.

1–2 December 2001 ▶ Major suicide bombings in Haifa and Jerusalem.

3 December 2001 ▶ Israel launches retaliatory strikes.

27 March 2003 ▶ Netanya suicide bombing – the 'Passover Massacre' – kills 30.

March–April 2004 ▶ The two co-founders of Hamas – Sheikh Ahmed Yassin and Abdel Azuz al-Rantissi – are killed by Israeli missiles.

25 January 2006 ▶ Hamas wins Palestinian National Authority elections.

democracy, yet here was a democratic election won by terrorists. Some claimed that the Hamas victory showed that addressing the real roots of conflicts by helping to resolve long-standing grievances was the most effective way of combating terrorism. The victory also created a dilemma for Hamas. It could either continue to support terrorist methods in pursuit of its aims, or it could act as a responsible government of the Palestinian territories. In fact, Hamas refused to renounce violence, recognize Israel's right to exist, or honour past peace agreements. In response, the USA, the EU, the UN and Russia imposed economic sanctions. A year after the elections, the sanctions remained in place.

CROSS-REFERENCE
MUSLIM BROTHERHOOD: PAGES **4–5**
SUICIDE BOMBINGS: PAGES **6–7, 40–41**

A Palestinian woman laments the loss of her apartment block, blown up by Israeli troops in revenge for a suicide bombing, September 2004.

'Long War' Speech

On 27 May 2006 President Bush delivered another important speech at the West Point Military Academy. Addressing the young, newly commissioned officers, he compared the war on terror to the Cold War against communism, which lasted for over 40 years. Like the Cold War, the new war with Islamic extremism would require 'the determination of generations of Americans'.

ASSESSING THE FUTURE

There were certainly no signs, in mid-2006, of an early end to the war on terror. In Iraq, the current 'front line' of that war, the number of terrorist incidents continued to rise. In Mumbai, India, an attack on several crowded commuter trains killed over 200 people in early July. Days later, the kidnapping of two Israeli soldiers by the Islamic extremist Hezbollah group triggered a sequence of terrorist acts by both sides that killed many Lebanese and Israeli civilians.

Perhaps most significantly, the victory in Afghanistan, which had kicked off the long-running war on terror, was showing signs of unravelling. Promises of international aid had fallen short and the defeated Taliban were increasingly active. Remnants of the old al-Qaeda leadership – including Osama bin Laden – remained at large in the border area. The authority of the Western-supported government led by Hamid Karzai barely extended beyond the capital Kabul, and even here its authority was in doubt.

One of several commuter trains in Mumbai, India, that were attacked by bombers on 11 July 2006.

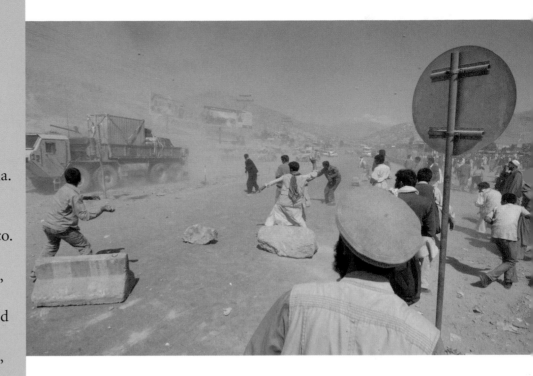

TIMELINE

MAJOR TERRORIST ATTACKS 2003–2006

12 May 2003 ▶ Suicide bombers attack Western compounds in Riyadh, Saudi Arabia.

16 May 2003 ▶ Series of suicide bombings in Casablanca, Morocco.

15 November 2003 ▶ Two synagogues are bombed in Istanbul, Turkey.

20 November 2003 ▶ British consulate and a British bank are bombed in Istanbul, Turkey.

11 March 2004 ▶ Explosives are detonated on four commuter trains in Madrid, Spain.

7 July 2005 ▶ In London, three underground trains and a bus are attacked by four suicide bombers.

9 November 2005 ▶ Three hotels in the Jordanian capital Amman are bombed.

11 July 2006 ▶ Several commuter trains bombed in Mumbai, India.

THE LONG ROAD AHEAD

On 29 May, two days after President Bush's speech, a crash caused by a US military vehicle resulted in several Afghan deaths. The anti-US riots that immediately followed claimed several more lives. Many observers were shocked by the depth of anti-Western feeling which welled to the surface after almost five years of relatively peaceful occupation. The struggle for hearts and minds in the Muslim world was clearly far from won.

Afghan demonstrators throw stones at a US military vehicle during the Kabul riots of 29 May 2006.

An alternative strategy?

'The greatest weapon available in the war on terrorism is the **courage, decency, humour and integrity** of the vast proportion of the world's 1.3 billion Muslims. It is this that is restricting the spread of "al-Qaeda" and its warped worldview, not the activities of counter-terror experts or the military strategists. Without it we are lost.'
From Jason Burke, *Al-Qaeda* (Penguin, 2004).

45

Key Figures in the War on Terror

ABDULLAH AZZAM (1941–89)

Abdullah Azzam was a Palestinian teacher who worked in many Middle Eastern countries. After the Soviet invasion of Afghanistan in 1979 he set up an agency in Pakistan to recruit Muslim fighters, and it was there that he met Osama bin Laden. In the late 1980s the two men created al-Qaeda as an international Muslim army, but they disagreed over tactics. Azzam was murdered in 1989, probably by friends of bin Laden.

GEORGE W. BUSH (1946–)

George W. Bush took office as US president in 2001. After 9/11, he created a coalition (union) of nations for the first stage of the war on terror: the military overthrow of the Taliban government in Afghanistan. Once he turned his attention to Iraq, however, this coalition began to dissolve, with many critics claiming that his administration was using the international war on terror as a cover for the pursuit of its own strategic and economic interests. The war against Saddam Hussein was successful, but the occupation that followed proved much more difficult. As a result Bush's popularity in the USA suffered a great deal.

SADDAM HUSSEIN (1937– 2006)

Sadam Hussein was president of Iraq from 1979 until 2003. His war with Iran (1981–8) bankrupted his country, and the invasion of Kuwait (1990–1) was reversed by a US-led coalition.

Despite the UN imposition of economic sanctions (limits on trade) he refused to cooperate with the international community, and was finally overthrown by another US-led army in 2003. After being found guilty of crimes against humanity, including the massacre of 18 Shia Muslims in the 1980s, he was executed in Iraq in December 2006.

OSAMA BIN LADEN (1957–)

Son of a Saudi construction company owner, Osama bin Laden became an Islamic extremist in his 20s, and travelled to Afghanistan to take part in the war against the Soviet occupation. After the Soviet withdrawal from Afghanistan in 1988, he and other Islamic extremists formed al-Qaeda to fight wherever it was needed. In 2001 he masterminded the 9/11 attacks on the USA, and has been the object of a worldwide manhunt ever since.

PERVEZ MUSHARRAF (1943–)

Musharraf was a general in the Pakistan army when, in 1999, he led a bloodless military coup that overthrew the elected government of Nawaz Sharif. In 2001 he appointed himself president. His support for the US-led war on terror was unpopular in Pakistan, where most people sympathized with the USA's opponents. Musharraf has managed to remain in power by obstructing the democratic process.

VLADIMIR PUTIN (1952–)

Vladimir Putin became president of Russia in 1999. He won popularity for his tough handling of the Second Chechen War (1999–2000) and has proved a strong supporter of the war on terror.

PAUL WOLFOWITZ (1943–)

Paul Wolfowitz held various positions under President George Bush (1989–93) and President George W. Bush (2001–). In the early 1990s he championed the ideas of a pre-emptive (strike-first) and unilateralist (US acting alone) foreign policy, and as Deputy Defense Secretary (2001–5) he helped turn these ideas into official US government policy (the Bush Doctrine). In 2005 he became president of the World Bank.

AYMAN AL-ZAWAHIRI (1951–)

Ayman al-Zawahiri, an Egyptian doctor and author, was head of the extremist Islamic Jihad group for many years before he merged the group with al-Qaeda to form the World Islamic Front for Jihad Against Jews and Crusaders. A prominent member of al-Qaeda since its early years, he is considered by many to be Osama bin Laden's deputy.

Glossary

anthrax bacterial disease in sheep or cattle which has been developed into a biological weapon against humans

civil liberties those freedoms of action and speech that are considered necessary for the proper functioning of a democratic society

coercion compel by use of force

Cold War name given to the hostility that existed between the free-enterprise capitalist and the communist worlds between 1947 and the late 1980s

containment preventing the expansion of a hostile country or its influence

freeze accounts prevent money from being paid in or taken out

intelligence services secret agencies that seek out information and try to counter enemies, both in their own countries and abroad

Islamic extremism the belief that (a) Islam should play a greater role in the way their society works, and (b) duty calls Muslims to defend the Islamic world from Western power and culture

militants people who are prepared to use aggressive action in support of their beliefs

neo-conservatives US politicians who believe in aggressively spreading US power and values

pre-emptive action attacking an enemy because you think the enemy is about to attack you

ricin deadly poison that can be refined into a powder or liquid and delivered as an aerosol spray, ingested or injected

Shia Muslims minority Muslim group worldwide, but the majority in Iran and Iraq

special forces small groups of soldiers with special skills

Sunni Muslims majority Muslim group worldwide, but a minority in Iran and Iraq

Taliban originally an Islamic student movement, the government of Afghanistan from 1996 to 2001

United Nations Charter constitution of the United Nations, which sets out the rules of behaviour between states

United Nations Security Council council within the United Nations most responsible for the maintenance of world peace and security. It has five permanent members – the USA, Russia, Britain, France and China – and ten rotating members that are chosen from other member states.

weapons of mass destruction (WMD) weapons capable of killing thousands, or laying waste large areas, at a single blow. They are usually subdivided into nuclear, chemical and biological weapons

Further Information

BOOKS

FOR CHILDREN

David Downing, *The War on Terrorism* (Heinemann Library, 2003)

Adam Hibbert, *What is Terrorism?* (Franklin Watts, 2002)

Alex Woolf, *Terrorism: The Impact on our Lives* (Hodder Wayland, 2005)

FOR YOUNG ADULTS

Jonathan Barker, *No-Nonsense Guide to Terrorism* (Verso, 2003)

Jason Burke, *Al-Qaeda* (Penguin, 2004)

Charles Townshend, *Terrorism: A very short introduction* (OUP, 2002)

WEBSITES

http://news.bbc.co.uk/1/hi/in_depth/world/2001/war_on_terror/
– a history of the war on terror in all its facets

www.genevaconventions.org/
– a reference guide to the Geneva Conventions, explaining the rules governing war and detention

http://www.cnn.com/WORLD/meast/archive/
– Middle East news from CNN, the USA's international news channel

http://english.aljazeera.net/
– news from the al-Jazeera network, giving an Arab point of view

Index

Numbers in **bold** refer to photographs.